JESUS
IS
EVERYWHERE

By Shauntae Spaulding

Jesus is Everywhere
Copyright © 2024 by Shauntae Spaulding

IBSN: 979-8-218-41144-2

www.spiritualgrowthministries.com

This book belongs to:

____

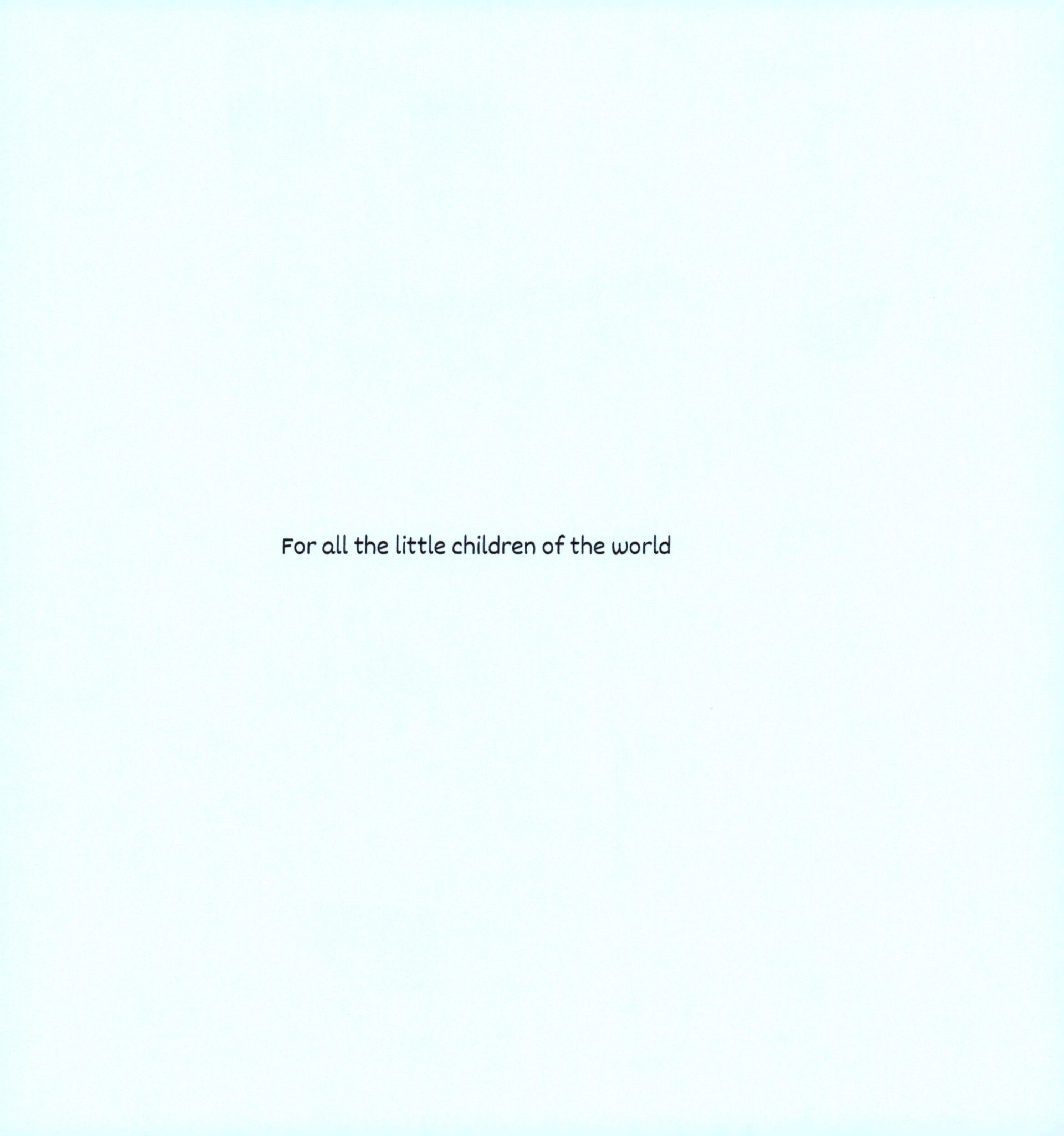
For all the little children of the world

ICE CREAM

you can't see Jesus
but he is here
he is with you
there is nothing to fear

you can see him everywhere
everywhere is true
just look at the things around you
you'll see him in everything you do

he is there when you wake up
he is there when you eat
he is there at the bus stop
even when you run down the street

looking at the flowers
or up in the sky
Jesus is everywhere
right as the bird's fly by

the squirrels up a tree
a dog in the yard
I see Jesus everywhere
no need to go far

in the mountains
or on a boat
he sits with me
as I drink a root beer float

at the park
or on a swing
he is with me
even in my dreams

Jesus is everywhere
everywhere is true
Jesus is everywhere
Jesus is with you

The End

About the Author

Shauntae Spaulding is a Christian single mother who resides in the San Fernando Valley with her son and adorable kitties. She enjoys connecting with others and sharing the love of Christ

You can find other publishing's and resources at:
www.spiritualgrowthministries.com